SPILLWAY

NEW AND SELECTED

Ian Pople was born in Ipswich and educated at the British Council, Athens, and the universities of Aston, Manchester and Nottingham. He has taught English in secondary and higher education in the UK, Sudan, Greece and Saudi Arabia. He taught at the University of Manchester for over twenty years.

SPILLWAY

NEW AND SELECTED POEMS

IAN POPLE

CARCANET POETRY

i.m. Roy Fisher

'Every turn of the tyre is a still point on the freeway.'
Fanny Howe

First published in Great Britain in 2022 by
Carcanet
Alliance House, 30 Cross Street
Manchester, M2 7AQ
www.carcanet.co.uk

Text copyright © Ian Pople 2022

The right of Ian Pople to be identified as the author
of this work has been asserted in accordance with the
Copyright, Designs and Patents Act of 1988; all rights reserved.

A CIP catalogue record for this book is
available from the British Library.

ISBN 978 1 80017 022 3

Book design by Andrew Latimer
Printed in Great Britain by SRP Ltd, Exeter, Devon

The publisher acknowledges financial
assistance from Arts Council England.

CONTENTS

New Poems

Grateful acknowledgment is made to the following publishers for permission to reprint from previous collections: to Arc Publications for permission to reprint poems from The Glass Enclosure, *1996*; An Occasional Lean-To, *2004*; Saving Spaces, *2011*; *to Flarestack Publishing for permission to reprint poems from* My Foolish Heart, *2006*; *to Rack Press for permission to reprint poems from* Silencing the Dust, *2013*; *to Melos Press for permission to reprint poems from* from The Evidence, *2018*; *to Anstruther Press, Canada for permission to reprint poems from* Spillway, *2020*.

.

SPILLWAY

NEW AND SELECTED POEMS

from THE GLASS ENCLOSURE (1996)

THE TREE LINE

There was the smell of water
sprayed in the late afternoon.
She stood on the other side
of the road looking up at pigeons,
as if scenting the air.

There had been cries coming
from the cloisters above the tree line.
Sounds in a language that,
in their separate lessons,
they had only just learned.

For him everything was changed,
he was the lover with a Casaubon tic.
Fascinated by her face, in his mind,
in the quiet house, he touched her body.
Looking out over the sea and holding

in his head those blues and golds
that cameras hold, as under ice
the calm trout waits for its displacements,
he wanted to run out amongst the shining cars,
rain beating on him from all sides.

BASLE

Behind me the garden descends to water.
Each night a balloon drifts over the river,
gas jets stain the silence
and trout rise into the shadows.

I watch the children through curtains
and weariness; this is the other weather,
a new carpet is laid, and the dogs run towards me
over gravel paths. 'No matter who it is

death is all these things and a release.
You know in all those years I only ever
changed trains there, once, in the middle
of the night.' Feet that kept on disappearing

as we walk towards the corner.
You stand beside the table.
As I put back the books, I get that
faint childhood smell of snow and urine.

WHEN THE SAINTS

1.

I was always killing something
on that road. First a rabbit.
Then a thrush flew up
into the windscreen. I had forgotten
the biology of Britain; that we, too,
have the pine marten and wild orchids.

I was like a free songbird.
The road ran beside a swollen river
and flooded field. I was looking for
that familiar spire lit by sudden sun;
the ingenuous smile you give me
as you turn to look out on the carpark.

We complete this room, your rationality
and mine merge and fill it up. My father
is getting as small and as brittle
as the memory of what they told me
was the Great North Road. We huddled
in my father's Morris and tall trees bent

over the road as the grey tarmac
dissolved in sunlight. Like
Russ Tamblyn cinematically miniaturised
as Tom Thumb, with his Irish friends
dancing among the trees, a chorea
has my father in the palm of his hand.

2.

Behind the screen of fields,
a film of clouds rolls endlessly.
Even the waterfowl fly up

over the roofs, the tarmac
and the seamless exhaust,
against the swell of the hill.

The clouds are tarnished
underneath. The water
does not weigh enough

for simple precipitation.
The tang of horses crops
his turf. The feet of ducks

never quite draw parallel
with the surface of his canals.
This mixture of exfoliation

and impediment: deafness,
the clinging chorea, a pacemaker.
As if I were the missing top joint

from the finger of his
right hand to show
where once I might have been.

THE BIG HOUSE

1.

As I spake unto you at that time saying
I am not able to bear you, myself alone,
the hand of the mason was taken and led

out into corridors of air, as much as
his feet shuffled over the paving stones
which are brought down and fallen

but we are made strong and stand upright.
On the Chapterhouse, Mr Gill's perspective
has shortened to an estuary where both eyes

move to a single side of the face.
The Christ Child is exposed to fumes
from Corporation Street and Deansgate.

St George genuflects and pouts at the Virgin.
St Denys in his mitre extends a finger
along his crozier towards the Hidden Gem.

'A bad site and an uncouth façade.'
Arm in arm with Pevsner, Pugin walks
inside, 'This building shows to what depths

even good men fall when they go whoring
after strange styles.' Our Lady of Manchester
is anorexic; souls have whistled through

her rib cage since the dawn of time.
They gather on the roof in Lowry's painting
and form the skyline into a set of candles.

Lowry's candles burn with a dark flame.
Souls have gathered in premonition of the Lord
to haunt Our Lady for the rest of her life.

2.

They had a lake in Trafford Park
and if it was fine on a Sunday
it used to be packed with people.
They used to walk to it, of course,
most of them. They had piano accordians
and ukuleles and all sorts going on,
it used to be great. There was
rowing boats and an island in the middle,
it was fantastic. In 1926 we went
to Blackpool for a week. My mother
used to scrimp and scrape and I was lucky.
Most children never even saw the sea.
You didn't get paid, not in those days.
You had to save up for that. I remember
being on the sands every day. You know,
having a ride on a donkey, an ice cream,
that sort of thing. Never more than a week.
By and large you'd go to a boarding house,
pay for the bed but you would provide
all the eatables. Later on when
I became an adult, my own holidays,
it shows how things had improved.
'Pack your baggage and truck to me,
we'll raise Cain and a family,
living in clover, thrilling all over with love.'
I had my name down for the big firm

at the time, Metropolitan Vickers.
They called it 'the big house.' To get
in there as long as you did your work
you know you were set for life.
12 streets and 4 avenues due to factories
all around. We were a little nation
of our own. We were Trafford Park.
When my wife got in and had a baby come
'Bugger off to work,' they says, 'You're
in the road. We'll do better than you.'
But they'd borrow a cup of sugar or an egg.
Marvellous people, marvellous people.

3.

See where Christ's blood streams above
Manchester. Pigeons settle in the interstices
of his toes and their dung and feathers
mottle his toenails. Flapping out into
August rain each of their pinions resounds

with the bells of his love. Above Ancoats
Hospital the box of a cantilever crane
brushes over his hair. To the ghosts
of horses that tramp the towing path
of the Bridgewater canal, the whole

of Trafford Park gleams in his assurances,
'Here is not heaven, Here is not
heaven!' On Palatine Road, Christian
shifts under his burden. Beside
the one-way traffic in Newton Street,

the authors of the apocryphal
Gospels shake out their umbrellas.
The blood of Christ mingles with
rain and mixes with detritus from
the city in the onrush to drains.

Under the streets, tunnels that
sighed with boredom, hug their
own hollowness. Christ's blood
streams in the firmament; take heed
that ye clamber too high or come

too near to the brink of the hill
called Error, for this is a by-way
to hell. The Pomona Docks are
neither soft nor workable. In
No. 1, a docker crushed between

a coal barge and a lighter, bleeds
his marrow into the nailed palms
of Our Lord. 'My Father on the Cross,
please take this anger from me
and draw me close to thee.'

Part two is a verbatim transcript from Dahrendorf on Britain; first
broadcast: Friday 7 January 1983, on BBC One London.

A SMALL TOWN IN THE SUDAN

1.

There is an autumn in the heat.
Yesterday she cut his hair in the garden,
and hair and small leaves spiralled
over the sand. In the sunset, a dog
moves from heat to heat among the refuse
on a corrugated roof as she comes
from the shower wrapped in a towel
and shaking her thin, wet hair.

Tonight, slender girls will pass their house.
Round their heads, scarves of black and gold,
of orange and brown, and on their heads
wicker trays. One of them will stop outside
the house and sit beside a hurricane lamp
and winnow peanuts. He thinks that she
will do this for forty years, and that already
she will have some particular way of twisting
paper funnels, of flicking peanuts so the least
amount is lost. His wife will dry her hair and
go out past card players under the tree –
they look up and straighten their white emmas,
their white jellabiyas – and she will give
the smiling girl crumpled money.

2.

'Syrians have been there for a hundred years.'
The women come to the cathedral,
with lowered eyes and stockinged legs

and stand among dusty leggy Dinka boys.
The men bring in the smell of shaving water,
sweat and cheap perfume. And in their neat,
clean shirts, they give a pound to each child,
and take ten themselves, to the collection box.
They feel they pay too much and never enough,
for children who lie on the floor and clap,
to nuns who stare and cajole.

3.

'We have a guava tree that gives one fruit
a week, if we can save it from the ants.
Every morning we look for scorpions
in our socks and ants shiver round the hole
down which we let the poison. One day,
the World Service brought us the voices
of Vietnamese in Ulster, voices coloured
with the Ulster vowels. I did not consider
that real, the hours of quiet in the afternoon,
or the English classrooms I had left,
or us together on the last flight home.'

---

emma: a white cloth wound around the head, *jellabiya*: a white robe,
Dinka: a Southern Sudanese ethnic group.

CAIN

I saw limes reaching through green
to yellow and apples began
to pick themselves. My hands

stiffened round the ropes but not
one furrow packed against another;
no robins, nor greasy ends

of broken worms over the shards
of the third day. My calloused heels
were cracked and micropore peeled off

into turning earth. The horizons
filled with sheep. I saw burning swords
unsheathed by cherubim and eyes

like owl's eyes in the sheep's heads.
Lamps were chasing night
over the moor and police cars spread

through Saddleworth. Those tapes
of him grunting through squat thrusts
and weights tumbling in bloody heaps.

FELLOW TRAVELLERS

The train begins our slow drive back
down through the bony mountains
to the cultivation of the valley floor.

Perhaps she feels herself a widow already,
clutching narcissi to her half-open coat,
and staring through the window,

like Sharaku's actor staring at the priest.
Perhaps there is a map among the trees,
in the stillness of the bird's head

is the movement of the stem it holds.
I lent boots to her quiet husband
and we crossed the fields to visit

the baptistry window; three hares
that dance endlessly in a circle,
and iron nails twisted in a crucifix,

the naked, halting fire of the man beneath;
to handle the book as if it were his own,
as if the marks there were made by him.

THE QUIET LIMITS

Lights swung from side
to side and mist settled
over the window where
light was calling on my skin.

I walked out into the shadow
of the church tower. I hold on
to things more satisfactorily
than you think; that moment

when the car kicks tram rails
and wrists give way. Then,
when you check the mirror,
the hand patting hair is yours.

THE SAME CONDEMNATION

There were not too many of us, I always thought
and I was always so glad of that,
that there were never too many of us.
It did, for example, at the very least,
grant an uninterrupted view of the river.

A crane like a single spider's leg.
And I imagine a man climbing
to the cab of the crane would wonder,
when he returned to earth, where was the earth.
And I never had the feeling, if I may use

so prosaic an image, of being the torn half
of a bus ticket, as I would surely have done
had there been more of us, and less uncertainty.
I have always found in my dealings with you
that a certain uncertainty has led

to a feeling of closer acquaintance;
a rather British feeling, one suspects,
in this day and age. And one that,
I hasten to add, I could not have shared
with the others. Not that they were

insensitive men; they were, each in his own way,
the very milk of human kindness,
whatever one might have read to the contrary,
and later. But uncertainty was their stock-in-trade
as it were, whereas I am, and always

have been, a rather nervous man,
susceptible always to the firm handshake,
the misted car, to Norrie's moments
for lightening the atmosphere, as much as
I recognised how that irritated James.

Huddled, as in a rainy bus-shelter,
amidst these uncertain friends, you yearn,
like the landlord's dog, for comfort.
And when the comfort of events was set
in train, I imagined us a set of boys

catching the bus to town, on a Saturday morning,
ground cigarette ash, bus breath
already half a morning used (my father
'Some of us work on Saturdays, you know.')
and further up the cambered top deck of the bus,

a single woollen glove. As it was,
these pictures were not too far from the truth.
For when we left the pub, they in their car,
we in ours, I had, as I have had before,
and dare say will again, a feeling

of running above the common-mill of things
as if I too sang in the outermost branches.
And this was so even as we crossed,
and recrossed the soft, illogical river,
to wait beside a lorry in a lay-by, its engine running.

GIFTS

We hold the eyelids down, dress
to fetch the midwife from four doors
down the same row of privies;
we use a sharp garland of words;
entry, snicket, alley and back.

To come in and out, to dress
a plain body on a plain bed
to soften and to fold in tissue,
dealt with by the cheque book
and the decent, kindly word, to seal

artifacts with the body; a picture,
teddy bears, rattles and ribbons
closed and fading under glass,
where smoky flames float on oil,
and every Sunday changes the flowers.

Take flowers or a plant to the host,
Not those peculiar biscuits
laid on window shelves for weeks
to smell of honey and dust; turning
flesh to stone and stone to words.

HUMBER DOUCY LANE

I collected up the windfalls and packed them
in a cupboard for the winter. They didn't keep
the taut smell of bark and musty autumn

but shrivelled and yellowed like the tapes
put round the trees to trap caterpillars
that climbed the trunks. I cut out

the middleman, took the fruit to grocers'
on the precinct and put a notice
on our gate. Mother said that I could

keep the money. But no-one came to buy.
In my shed, fifty yards from the house,
dried spiders and a drumkit replaced

the chemist's bench and tubes; gas-jars
I brewed oxygen in to flare magnesium strips;
the whole hut and the orchard brightened.

As instructed by my teachers, I turned
my head away. Years afterwards, our neighbour,
Mrs Johnson, splintery with Alzheimer's,

walked naked up and down the lane. Her Labrador pup,
hit a glancing blow by a car on Rushmere Road,
pulled weakly from his basket to lick my face.

AT THE NAVIGATION

The sun was tucked behind the visor
as I was driving back from work;
the road reached round from house

to house. A horse was grazing
an out-of-season cricket pitch.
They were leading sheep down

to the reservoir; hooves slipped
from bank to crumpled sky; fleecy heads
bobbed out towards the middle.

Parish boundaries widen
every year; another heart attack,
another priest who's irreplaceable,

whose altar glides to silence.
And half a mile below the crinkly spine
of England, a couple leg their boat

and feel, from the neighbouring tunnel,
the pulse of a train tearing
towards the whole of Europe.

FOR JON, PAM, TOM AND KATIE UP IN THE AIR

1.

Here there is no memory palace;
no warriors locked in combat
in the southeast corner
of the reception hall;

in the northeast corner
there is no Xixia woman
who is huihui. Only this,
that after the plane had rolled

to a stop, the faces in the aisles
with bags, brushes and hoovers,
busy in the toilets, recapping
hand lotion, washing toilet bowls.

And in their memory palace?
A crown prince at the gaming tables.
All of that that is farang and this
is what we keep even to ourselves,

unless we trust the farang
with the precious things
that are not theirs and can
only be trusted with them.

*

'Let us take a tuk-tuk into the foul air.'
So, Jenny leaping from the chair
she sat in. The children in the hotel care.

Their sleep is smuggling down the intercom.
The hotel nurse who looks just twelve
with ten years in the Gulf and lucky

to be here right now. Like us as we pitch
on three wheels from Soi Carboy to Patpong
and clutch each other even tighter.

English – off to where women smoke
cigarettes with their vaginas and then blow
paper darts through cardboard tubes.

'It was like being hypnotised. He showed me
a piece of silk I didn't really want
and couldn't really afford. Then he did

that draping bit and started telling me
what it did for my eyes and my hair
and the next thing I knew, I was out

on the street with three and a half yards
of the damned stuff.' A house with walls
with walls turned inside out

so the carvings face the diners.
And where is the ivory mouse palace?
Somewhere up the stairs and on the left.

*

And if something terrible happens,
something not unlike a sudden,
mighty wind. Simonides, among
the passengers, will remember

the exact positions of the relatives
and friends, aisle or window,
as his eye blinks the cursor;
business class, smoking.

For here, in the toilet of the memory
palace, the hand lotion is finally
uncapped and its pink lines run along
the toilet walls and across the ceiling.

3.

Leaping over the Pearl River
cost him a broken ankle
and a limp for the rest
of his days; catching the metro
took a minute, two dollars
and enough left for another pair

of cloisonné vases.
The world's longest escalator
takes you well away
from screaming Boat People
and wet ropes slopping wood.
Children of six and seven

play inside the Walled City;
no more walled than you or I,
'I mean, it was a million
to one chance we'd walk past
that shop again and then
she dashed out to tell me

she'd been through the whole shop
and found the matching one.
And so, after that, I had to buy it.'
Wet hawsers slap the Walled City.
It pitches in its own mind,
yawing through the forty-five degrees

of the spirits of the ancestors.
Lines of washing slide from balconies
toward the loosening horizon.
Sixty-six stitches across his back
hold together the zany ideogram
of his knife wounds. The girls

and their numbers are chosen
by customers through a grille.
All of them slip a little further
into kilter and the permanent rain;
a splinter of bone then pierced
the right kneecap. As they attached

a metal brace to stop his right leg
shrivelling shorter than his left,
a vision of Mary and her child
left his heart serene and his flesh
finally untroubled by lust.
Ropes tighten into the sea;

and all of Aberdeen twinkles at night
from the top of the world's longest
escalator until it takes the rapids
at full sail and in a moment
is turned over and spun round
along with two other ships

in which are travelling
the mandarin's possessions.
Thus did I and João Barradas
get sent to the Bottom. But God
aided me because I caught hold
of some Rope which by Divine

Providence I found between my Hands
and was able to pull myself
onto a Support of the same Ship.
But João Barradas went to the Bottom
and the Current carried him away
and he never reappeared.

4.

It was the pecking of a single bird that made
the hardened ground throw up all of this;

the car tracks and the stiffened marks of rain.
From reed beds threaded with empty cans

and plastic cups, the koala yawns up
into old light and shakes off the dust.

He remembers pissing on the Minister of Tourism
just a week before they handed him to Tom

and lurches off into the untravelled, unnamed
nothing. Both he and Cook create the space

that runs between the landmarks. There is no name
without a place. We'll leave most of that

to Mr Hawkesworth and the Endeavour journals;
their genius for the matter of fact and to those

who followed Cook; always filling in,
always disappointed, consecrating

a system of differences in the idea of land.
And that was only the third car between

here and Dubbo and I thought, Poor sister,
poor sister. The tennis court run to earth.

The fly screen round the verandah all
shot through, the team house left

to the visiting team. But the two rooms
where they lived, she kept them very clean.

With flowers more architectural than pretty,
the continent had shut its shell before the songlines

crossed the Torres strait. The rivers run to nothing.
Casuarinas mesh the sun. Sea wasps love us all.

The world's largest stone. Two-thirds below the ground
though how would you know. Thousands there

– you wouldn't notice. So, on the first anniversary,
in front of the marble mausoleum the men shiver

and weep. And in a souk she has known for thirty years
a perfect stranger comes to tell her, 'Mrs Mann.

I'm very sorry. Your husband is dead.' So,
with the eucalyptus mist of the Blue Mountains

scented with urine, and with a stock of dialects
from Narragin to Wearside, Tom and the koala

clutch a boomerang and a cabbage tree hat,
turn to slam the kitchen door and go back in.

from AN OCCASIONAL LEAN-TO (2004)

1.

What moves before surf
in the tide are filaments
and lucid flesh, a swollen
green; particle and wave
hidden in debris that longs

to be ice. Water is litter
worn from itself, from
continents in absentia,
subsistence farming
of matter. As we take

steps to hold what fluid
means in us, so the parachute
canopy becomes the plane
and the car, a lean-to
under splintering sky.

*

Small boy in a red hat
saw chaffinches, fungi,
a tree-creeper, butter bur,
and learnt to prise them
from his wildlife book.

We bent to bitter florets
of marsh marigold.
Anglers, hand over hand,
gathered skittering fish that
warped away from themselves

unable to recede to a light
they had only just been,
between carpet mill
and empty football ground,
in this pivot of water.

*

Driving past on the top
road, the wipers slow;
the self is uncertain,
untranscended,
an iron taste in the mouth.

Birds in white-grey
sky are filaments
of a darker world. Crows
on the unsettling twig,
rooks in vortices

of cantilevered flight
are perhaps versions
of the go-between god;
the certain pigeon, a swallow
flying from the early plough.

*

This valley is distinct
and warm, made from ash,
conifers, laburnum,
crazed with paths
that sheep have cut.

The heron is open above
and apple blossom below;
though somewhere near
an engine seems to be
drowning. And this

is the testament, how
that sub-frame became
stranded beyond the field
gate and the plum tree
espaliered into life.

*

It means we take
the three good symbols,
wood, blood and water,
in a metal wheelbarrow
along the lawn edge,

as the yellowhammer
shortens our view
from birdfeeder to shrub;
green against red,
yellow against blue,

the colours sing and rise,
one above another.

The blue is pristine,
receding, but always
within the frame.

*

To think of that dance
of hands in a small, oak-
panelled committee
room as memory,
where the door opens

to a draft that catches
transparent plastic
and runs it across
the concrete floor
of an Anderson shelter,

or a church, its smell
censed clean, a woman
kneeling in the undercroft;
the difference between
being and becoming.

2.

The scene bisected
by a single point
of light which comes
in time from above,
on skin contained

in hair or clothing,
touch in a dark room.
A rook in daylight,
the Little Owl at dusk,
their wings opened

over pavement
where the fleece is dry
but the ground is wet,
or the ground is dry
and the fleece is wet.

*

This is the wool and this
the shorn sheep. Trees,
in sprays of light, sway
out from the valley side
that tips to the tidal edge.

This is the pigeon and this
the quivering squab. At ebb
the inlet is a straggle of skin
where trees close
on oyster catchers and the knot.

This is the church and this
the naked sky. All this
from the pub, a hundred feet
above tide pools,
the estuary's assertions.

*

Not the ghost of itself,
but a gate-leg table
opened out for breakfast
in an angle of light
that turns under the eye.

Not the candle repeating
the flame, or pheasants splashing
to roost, or fox fire
among rotted branches
an hour beyond dusk.

But as if the newly dead
were to gather and tell
a single story or
blow cigarette smoke
towards the sharpening moon.

*

Tumbled chairs,
that awkward fervour
traced back and forth
over gesso;
always immanent

but liable to
culverting,
enforced decay,
the misperceptions
of analogy,

and the challenge
of that early light,
hardly florid
but there still between
the icon and the pixel.

3.

The function of this pond
is apprehension;
both torque and bowser.
For, beneath the surface,
under moving dust,

the sunlit water snail
spreads its foot
and beetles seethe
in their own bubbles,
and what come across

most strongly is
the clear possibility
of water plaiting
and unplaiting down
the backs of furniture.

*

Suddenly, from the adit,
a hare, pelting as if
for its life, along
the muddied runnel, past
the wash trough, across

the moor towards the beck;
no interiority
then, no chance
to metastasize
beyond the passive voice

or the taking of chances,
as, under the wonderful
flight path of ducks,
a dead bream buckles
to the canal surface.

*

Water-dark clouds over
urgent water where flood
debris has cushioned
the appetites of flood.
On barbed wire, leaves

hung with stream spray
and, on dun-coloured
aggregate, a new light
come to stabilize
those pale images

of something slewed
quickly from gouged grass
beside the bypass,
a strewn pain, pith,
a streak of new earth.

*

At the lake edge,
that sparse evening
of drizzle and mosquitoes,
she had stepped
from the moored boat

and set it rocking.
There was a hand, palm
out, inside
the wet windscreen.
In the photograph,

she neither looks
nor does not
at the camera.
She went away
and there was nothing.

*

This baptism, a stone
blebbed with itself
as if newly fired,
among lithe tongues
of hostas or pelargoniums,

that keeps the early sun.
A test of silent unities
allows us to give voice.
Autumn spate on a stream
that runs by new housing,

under the road, behind
the Methodist chapel,

village bakery and red-
brick terrace; its need
for yet another breath.

*

All the way along,
the sun shone on
the undersides of leaves
and angels couldn't trick
you out of it;

the campsite smell
of warm rain, dusk
and grass; a quiet voice
as a hand rubbed canvas,
and in the river's surface

an insect buzzed
to its death and dead
might be lit from below;
a microscope slide
of limbs and old habits.

*

Taut light has gathered
around this place
between the Hudson
and the Poughkeepsie bridge.
White clapboard house

among fir trees,
a habitation for grace,

a word and past enough.
Our fingers dabbled,
careless and quick, upon

the rowed boat's wake.
A summer rain storm
shakes the swimming pool
and, behind that voice,
the sound of yet another.

*

From the cliff top
to the rocks below, the still
and deepening sea,
where fingertips can find
a place that is not

land or water,
where a rib cage is
and below that, skate
and seakale, nutrients
that are vestments

too, for near all
this are coastal towns
where seagulls
scream and dawdle over
waiting Sunday streets.

*

The duckboard dips
to the surface beneath,

each touch annealed,
cramped in faith,
where we step over

suspended matter,
foul water and mud,
the ground of our being
in so many ironies
that balance our way

to a green hide among
reed beds to witness
the Grey Lag Goose
loosen from water and lift
towards the giddy limits.

*

January cloud
and sky without rain
but full of purpose.
Winter steps, mud
and dark leaves

caught against risers.
Footprints frozen
in mud; elsewhere
cycle tracks set
in gelid grass.

Memorial Gardens;
in the bandstand,
the guttering's loose

or gone, the ceiling
flakes in rosettes.

4.

A place not in
our racial history
not fully brought
to self-consciousness;
beyond fire and smoke,

beyond the parterre,
the walled garden, sheep
lying on the drive,
reed beds and a heron
rising to mobbing rooks,

field and hedgerow,
taut horizon,
gathering distance;
this string of events
where silence is.

*

In the place are
the 1950s,
that walked a hospital
corridor in
late sunlight.

In this place are
the 1960s,
that lay under a tree
with bougainvillea
on a south facing wall.

Think of Laocoon
wrestling the serpents
with and for his
sons, a tall order,
another crucifixion.

*

Moss on old slate,
lichen smears and fungus.
Excluded under the soffit,
a snail reads the surface
with its fondling slime.

Between render and stucco,
out of chafing winds
enough seepage to deter
the final autumn wasp
fresh from the soul of crowds.

Wasp and snail who
make their testimony
among prefabs,
hutments and leaf smoke
at the ragged civic edge.

*

What remained after
the house burned, the lawn
in silence and smoke drift,
was a compost bin,
eggshells, rot,

cabbage stalks and flies
rising and settling. That
afternoon when
the stream ran on
by chemical pools

and security cameras,
between culverted sidings,
the motorway and Steel
works; the tongue left
to search behind the teeth.

*

At eight o'clock, the horses
came, animal and rider
in day-glo coats, between
pavement maples. They
came towards the sleep

of horses, where horses
kneel or stand those
hours among the impulses
of dream. What grainy
imagery might that be

to which a human
could contribute:
tiltyard and flag,
smoke and early sun,
metaphor and habit?

5.

Here's the church and here's
the steeple; here's the priest
and here are the people
and there, on the tarmac,
are toy people who

make tiny gestures
or walk among planes
or drive model cars.
And there are those
who have been taken

from their own lives
and those whom we
know to be in
someone else's
clothing and skin.

*

A red calorgas
cylinder in a doorless
trackside shed with
buddleia and the ghost
of a passing train would

imply such and such
a human body or hill
slope under the form
of pencil and paint
that had become the portion

of goods given which
is forgiveness
and emulation,
drizzle on a slate roof
on a winter afternoon.

*

Without the doll's house
which her father made,
which was her house
and beyond it, is
the darkness, unreturned.

Between sunset
and sunrise when
her hair was scraped
back and her mouth
wounded, a fly became

a nest of eggs, and the doll's
house offered more
and more light. At once
her father was both
lost and found.

*

But look, it is winter,
she is old in sleep,
will do the cold thing
and stay away; the drizzle
of torment designed

to catch herself
unawares and will
not remove the splinters
from under her nails;
watches for encroachment

of all measure of dignity.
The pestle resting in chaff
and uncrushed grain, she
waits for the veil to rend,
rend to the last tatter.

*

To draw a portrait
of desire where
mystery decays
to belief is to ask
why this white

concrete box partly
bitten back to the steel
reinforcement was pitched
on its side among marram
grass by a coastal path

or a hanging basket
is a gash of blue

from a car and yet on
foot is the usual mix
of lobelia and petunias.

*

The monastery sat. Its
blue dome bobbed
against the pines, outside
were cannons, a restless
flag. Below were rocks,

a still and deepening
sea. Across the inlet,
there they stood,
the king and queen among
the muscular horses

on the hill. But who owned
them and the beasts they
walked among and birds
that flickered up and off
as they walked on?

6.

From allotment skies
July showers fall
to rouse young crows
on dusty branches.
The fat earth buckles.

Samuel Palmer knew
how each leaf lies
clear of the next
in wind-held sun
where hover flies float,

the stark implications
of trees at hand, their
canopy's calm belief
in time - this week
and the week after next.

*

Has nothing changed?
Japonica rises beside
the basement window,
where a crane fly
feels cold air. There

are hands that seem
to touch the child, neat,
distressed with the very
borders of affliction.
From the wainscot, the

printed paper, mouldings,
a coffered ceiling, and
clarifying skies
where gliders turn
beneath a private sun.

*

Winter comes beside
the railway. Through
it you can see the things
that summer hid:
the nuanced English

countryside that spreads
out from the train, horses
bent to grazing, a hiker
squeezing by two
concrete posts

to look beyond that
gate, at understory
and coppicing, to each
indifferent east
and all the other souths.

*

A bundle of wood, a web
of aconite were left
beyond the measures
that produced the sarabande
and the gavotte, as then

the collared dove
settled on bark chippings
in the darkness of
the solemn underbrush.
Forms of life that seem

to merge with rocks at dusk
live with the moon
behind them, as under-
water are the mollusc
and unblinking fish.

*

Three kinds of litany:
one faithful and revealed,
one traditional
and another that works
against its mooring

through a summer
of floods and ragwort,
until a warm September
of bramble and blackberry
when what dies back

from the river side
is a return to earlier
voices that sang, open-
throated and unbearably,
of the way things are.

*

To walk the grain of the field
in the wind rush of grass
and follow a rising arc
to the white edge and beyond;
to trace the pattern of speech.

These are new scents
for the upland hare, above
a stream on sheep pasture
among rank bracken
and sliding stone. To ripple,

complete the shadow
that shapes behind rock,
complete and then
turn back to the start,
each strand, each wave.

from **MY FOOLISH HEART (2006)**

TURNING THE TABLES

Across the valley, lights burn
in houses where children return from school
with the smell of winter and elusive stories;

men listen to engines turning
and the World Service. Newels, joists
and lintels swell in the hedge bottoms.

When he turned her onto her stomach,
he saw stars scattered on the sheets,
felt movement in his fingertips.

ATHENS

at pantograph level:
energy low but pitched
to the quarried skyline,
white shorn upon blue
that takes up the pleasantries
of perspective, brings
an Alsatian from the eighth floor,
the winch gear threading
open space and closed;

at Pericles' level,
stares out to Piraeus;
cats on warm balconies
among cage birds,
the sound of a woman
in black-rimmed glasses
listening, in the mid-afternoon,
to high heels crossing
the marble floor above;

and would know that,
below the Parliament building,
under awnings, tables
and slatted uneven chairs,
islanded by airport buses
and yesterday's foreign papers,
small steps to a gesture
are jigsawed into place
with coffee in tiny cups,
the grounds plush with sugar
and the overhead sun.

to Edmund Prestwich

SPEAKING TERMS

From a lift where the light emerges
from above the mirror and when the doors
pull open you always turn to the left,
over red-brown carpet so worn in places
the underfelt shows and where, you know,
years of cleaners have never hoovered
deep enough into the angle between pile
and wainscot; there is a smell of drying out
and crumbling. And past a ply and plasterboard
door, that's always scuffed and worn
around the handle, the man expecting you
is sitting. You would have liked him to be
shorter than you as he rises from his chair
to greet you, with receding hair and glasses,
but instead he's taller and slightly stooping
with the bluest eyes you have seen
since you met the playwright's nephew.
And it's no good asking why you
are here, because, you see, there is
a little crisis just around the corner
in Lesotho or Belize, somewhere
in this known and shrinking world,
and it's no good saying that you were there
only to teach and that was years ago
and with the British Council, because
the thought of open sky five floors
above your head and the bus ride
through the evening crowded autumn streets
won't help you breathe. As if the walking
from a smoky staffroom to another lift
had been enough to rouse you for the act

of teaching. But scuffling pupils
running to the classroom and pushing past
has just depressed you in unexpected ways.
Perspective now is down through wormless earth,
almost to the molten core and you would like
to need to pull the collar from around your neck,
or fish your hankie out to wipe your brow
but it's not true and all the time the face
has gone on talking, far, far more
than you had had the right to hope and the print
of some small copse in somewhere English
that's behind him on the wall has faded to its frame
and silence then sets in. Suddenly, a voice
that's yours begins to talk you through
the problems and you're writing for yourself
a memorandum of understanding and there's
the pulling back of chairs, the proffered hand.
The hollow office door is closing shut
behind you and the dozen little marionettes
that voice your life are clustering round you
asking for your help. Light falls from plastic
boxes where dead moths have gathered.
So you avoid the lift and take the concrete,
cold stairs up, and cross the concrete foyer
through swing doors into autumn light.

THURSDAY MARKET

Three boys bargain for a pigeon.
They spread the wings, work slowly
down the throat; awkward and tender,
each haruspex bends to the vent's
soft gleam. The pigeon's thrown
to the end of its tether. Others,
beside themselves with each other
in wire lobster pots, are nuzzled
to the peering faces where exhaustion
spools from bird to boy to dust.
The squabs are either naked,
plucked and trussed for eating,
or feathers spread by rain or death.
The palm trees are diseased, bottom
branches hang uncradled, fruit
in haemorrhoidal bunches shrivels
and falls. Water troughs dry
to concrete and wood, warp and split
into the sand. The paving has buckled.
From it dwarf palms rise to sharpen
their leaves and crowd the road.
A dozen lovebirds flit together
in a single cube of air. The parakeets
are knuckled to their perches,
defeated by heat, their crest
knocked awry against the wire.
The mynah's chocolate sheen
is crazed with its own mute,
a sliver of skylight in its alien eye.

He waited for the doors to bang
behind him but the wind
gusted him like paper
over the trees and he forgot
even his children's names.
Their round faces giggled
up to him, but he thought
they were sparrows sidling
along the gutter. Gulls,
like lifting feet, trickled
their ghosts over ploughed
fields. As we walked
the unattended streets,
onto the empty platform,
he leant us his face;
it came bowling along
after him over the rails.
The moon swung the night
smoothly round us and we spun
the tiny light of ourselves
among the empty bus-stands.
But he had tricked us all,
had dragged us into the dark,
slammed the door behind us,
and settled the gulls again
around the silent harrow.

THE SCATTERING SCREE

And on the edge, rooks on thermals
over us, we stand in the valley floor.
Under scree, a broken stream bubbles
and behind us rolls the sky.

We walk on to the house beyond
and wait inside the kitchen as others
talk by the long table, gather food,
go to set ponderous log fires

in bedrooms or the empty library.
Then they follow, scatter goats
with their laden donkeys, fire a flare,
clatter the pale moraine in modern boots.

THE COLLAR

He came to the morning grate in the cold hearth
Where faded blue tiles had crackle picked out
With swept ash. He riddled the grave clinker,
Collected it on a shovel and wrapped it fatly
Into paper, carried it above the carpet to where
The back door, blue, took early morning sun,
And frost had starched the lawn, came back
With feathery kindling, took an old *Mirror*
And, ripping the pages, crumpled it into a ball.
He put the longer wood, six by half-inch lengths
Of old shed door, or dismantlings from inside
The clanging Anderson shelter, into a stack
Around the paper, and struck an acrid match.
We watched the pale grey wisp against the soot
As the wood too fire along its splinters.
He placed coal from the metal blue scuttle
And the smoke swelled warm then must.
A small rivet at the back of his shirt
Had caught the shiny, detachable collar.

As men and women left the train
and moved into the segments of their lives,

I left that station for the first time,
the evening newly darkened,

and then walked streets I'd walked
before, neon drifting pavements,

Enville Street, Penny Meadow, and went
to my appointment. I thought of your

new intentions and how the rails
spill on until they touch real presences –

beyond sleepers and aggregate sopped
with oil, scorched buddleia, brambles,

the tunnel entrance and the hill's brow,
and that angel caught in mid-utterance.

BOOTH HALL CHILDREN'S HOSPITAL

To Ben

It was not bruised light on the tricycles
or the Subbuteo baize reminded me of where
I was, but waking in the lean-to play room,
the duvet sliding off me on the truckle bed,
under Perspex brocaded with green fungus.

And someone in the ward felt strong, as daylight
sashayed through the happy curtains, a chair moved
by itself between two beds. They were emptying
our little boy before his operation; above his head
a hand scrawled note read, 'Nil by mouth'.

They spent a long time trying to find a vein;
when Sister said that there were easier veins in babies' heads,
my wife's face leant into her hands and tears
squeezed themselves between her fingers.
'What a temper!' Sister said about the baby.

The registrar was haunted by his tailor;
fresh faced, public schooled, his sharp jacket
parried all our questions until I blew my top.
The women in the parent's room wore fluffy mules,
quilted dressing gowns, black eyeliner

and were mostly bleached blond. They ordered pizza
into the small hours and wouldn't stop smoking.
There was a just a single 'get-well' card for Ben
and that was from the Mother of the cot next door
in the ward that they'd just moved us from.

In the other cot the babies came and went.
One was dark-haired, chubby, hydrocephalic,
his forehead buckled by a fracture. Only he
knew how to play; his parents sat in flaming
silence, his mother mute with anger.

Nurses made Josh special, sang and held him;
at eighteen months, he fed through a wine tap
in his stomach and focussed on nothing.
He mewed and squealed at birds he saw
and played cat's cradle with no string.

In that feeble March we'd take Ben out
into the park, in a heavy, elderly pram,
its C springs sighed and whistled to the ducks.
The anglers catapulted maggots to the fish
and waited for the scruffy lake to yield.

At seven pm, the night staff gathered, chiaroscuro
by the angle-poise, an inflated cartoon rabbit
floated in and out of light above them.
A drip machine called from darkness by a bed,
was attended, readjusted, calmed and stilled.

Our son was quiet again. Laundered curtains cut
one darkness from another, between them
I could see, beside the outside Perspex doors,
two men, vague, particoloured, faces thrawn
in poor light, nubbing out their cigarettes.

PIANISM

However much
the soft pedal
tiptoed, he took it
all to heart. It took
the whole shape of him
and loitered on his skin
in the perfume
of a long set
in a smoke-filled club
or the shape of sleep
on the back seat
of a cab as the road
settled into chord changes
all the way to Albany

from SAVING SPACES (2011)

FOR THIS RELIEF, MUCH THANKS

The magpies and the seagulls fly up here
and other darker, fleeting birds that glide
past roofs with railings, satellite dishes,
clock towers above hotel conversions,
the clouded background. Down there,
grass, a mulch of fallen leaf, people
waiting. Behind me, my appointment.

A THOUSAND TWANGLING INSTRUMENTS

You might as well pray
for the cyclist to bend under
branches by the dull canal.
You might as well pray

for the bramble to slink back
away from the allotment path
and the strawberries to compete,
for the boy to hold the kite

above the generous sea-taut rocks,
the water breaking its black and blues,
for easy imprecations and
the grey moth that walks the page.

A WEEK OF RUNNING BESIDE THE CANAL

On Monday, three yellow goslings
and the gander's tongue thrust out.
On Wednesday, three goslings
each with a dark Mohican streak,
the gander's tongue thrust out.

A face comes back from
earlier times, freckled, round,
brown eyes and red, fair hair,
nothing beyond the ordinary,
that always seemed relaxed.

The gait below it, slightly
splayed and rolling.
On Thursday, suddenly
the may was open everywhere,
its small, white clusters

like the rowan or cow parsley,
the florets twisted, flicking
in the breeze. On Sunday,
one upon the water, its head
tucked back under its wing,

the other adult bird
was resting by the bank,
the water rippling its
drowned head. Of
the goslings, nothing.

On the canal, warm dots
of summer rain. Friesians
walk among the grasses.
That face opens out upon itself.
The bee's feet touch the flower.

SET ELEMENTS FOR JOHN BROWN — ISAMU NOGUCHI

I will return for the coat
           hanging above the hat.
I will return for the noose
hanging above the coat.
But first, I will take the hat
and look hard at those three twigs,
the wood they are set in
           and the horizon they will always be.

All these things so swiftly
built, the sage panopticon
-Kilmainham, Pentonville,
the grey expanse of wall,
its shadows. And then,
'Forget the left eye, see only
with the right,' that seahorse
dead and dried; beneath
the cassock, feathered feet,
since that might be the thing
that's brought us here;
if you have that expression
in your mouth, I'll use it too.

OWL

Stubby Venus on stubby-fingered wind,
that flapped above a childhood park,
a rail to somersault on over gravel.
Firm-winged familiar, that winter of 63,
the sledge so slow over the last snow,

it sent in Father – old nicotine fingers,
wheezy-cackle breath – among the cat-ice
and pine-needles, worn earth, root balls,
worm death. We saw him glide
into the tree silhouette and not emerge.

THAT DAY

That day,
          stuck as I was
                    in the town
watching my feet
          slide on the snow
                    on the slope,
I came upon the thing
          that I was,
                    a gull, speckled,
brown, juvenile,
          facing the closed door
                    of the bingo hall,
turning,
          occasionally,
                    to glance
at the people
          walking past,
                    as I was.

THE BLEACHERS

You were running over snow,
snow over the playing field.
Your feet were kicking up

snow in arcs from your heels.
You did not see, how could you see
thin chains hung with snow

between thin, white posts
until you were pulled from
beneath yourself, your hair

splintering not so very far away
in the raw wind. What did
the others see from the edge,

those with small dogs tucked
under their chins with their scarves
thinking of shop fronts and grey skies

over winter beaches, grey skies
over bleachers, those skies
over concert halls that listen

to the end of the cadenza,
to the gathering applause,
the applause coming to an end?

FROM THE SHEARER AND THE LAMB

1. [6 v 05]

Above the roof-tree is
sky in torment where
birds rage and angels,
huddled against the storm,

wait for a gap in the clouds
to hold their harmonies.
Beneath our feet, an earthen
floor is strewn with thyme.

Then the ocean-filled
basement, scuffed waves,
darkened yachts with riding
lights, the taut leviathan.

2. [6 v 05]

Snow from Spring sky
rests and melts. Alder
pollarded along the ditch.
The ex-grammar-school boy

tamps his pipe with fat thumb.
His plot, his allotment
where last year a wasps' nest
stalled in the redcurrant.

When its neophytes pulled

clear of the deft cells,
convolvulus struck it down
with seething skill.

3. *[6 v 05]*

That day was their first use
in the whole time since
his father's death, eleven years
before; the mute swan

and the whooper, avocet
and teal, tufted duck and lapwing,
the pochard and the redshank;
pushing the eyepieces closer

and apart, that occluded,
needed to be refocused;
shoveler duck and egret,
marsh harrier, bunting.

4. *[20 vi 05]*

His father drove round
flat East Anglia surveying
lifts and chains; if he
hit a pheasant, he would

stop to pick it up or
lose it to the car behind.
So when a pigeon clapped
into the Hull express

emerging on the up-line,
the feathers slip-streamed,
settling silently apart,
he wasn't much surprised.

5. *[30 vi 05]*

Inside a drawer, a banana
blackens. In the empty room,
a house plant flicks,
adjusts its darkening leaves.

The driver waits. The hand-
brake is released. The car
lifts from the curb. So a trout,
in mild water, waits below

the slight spillway, waits
for spate to release
the drain, the spindrift,
brilliant, temporary, brash.

6. *[nd.]*

What could be made
of Cavafy; who loved
the church for its silver
vessels, its light and icons,

the conventions of liturgy;
who loved the eparch's

son for the hair on his
forearm and the wait

that occasioned; the grey-
lidded harbour rocking
with autumn light
and still untrodden?

7. [nd.]

He bought himself some
red and white canvas,
cut a window in the front;
made a swazzle, practised

so it didn't rasp his palate.
On his right hand
was Mr Punch, who named
the others: Judy, the crocodile,

a string of sausages. He
practised hanging the Beadle,
kept on repeating,
'That's the way to do it.'

8. [18 vii 05] to Fr. Stan Dye

A man as a locked bundle
of rods, a man's joints
welded in bronze, eye
sockets where fingertips

search, cheek hollows stubbled
with swarf. Even then,
if the man won't reply, the maker
can threaten to evict the voice,

stop it quickening into conduit,
and tip him over, into the forest
litter, among beech husks
and blackbirds turning leaves.

9. *[4 xi 05]*

The corner of a horse-field,
with open half-garages,
a magpie coming in, low
over the flat roofs. The smell

of pruned cypress made them
feel at home for a moment,
when they were in love:
when they emerged from

the weekend hotel with eyes
slightly glazed, and turned
along the High Street
for one final photograph.

10. *[5 iii 06]*

A pitched place, arrived at
from below, it looks across

the plain. In dust corners,
between the adze and the chaff,

they debate abandonment;
finding in winter, a new
here; in summer, a new
there. So the meltemi

will soften the afternoon
and dogs bark at sunset,
where hens scratch
the strange, anticipating earth.

11. *[7 vi 06]*

Turn him inside out and
lay his muscles out
upon his skin, turn
him to face the other way.

Lay open the flaying
fist, lay open the stream
in spate, lay open
his love and stream it

in another's tears, for I
saw her lying under him
and the one occupying
and completing the other.

WINTER

Winter is a sacrament:
the solitary bee has hidden among the splinters
the crow, up there in the long forest, shakes off the rain
the pig stands in its fleece of steam
the pipistrelle nudges deeper in the tree cleft,

and He has looked on it and confidently stated,
        'This is my deposit',
the heart with its old-fashioned indigo.

from SILENCING THE DUST (2013)

THREE BAGATELLES

I.

The bark came slowly away from the branch,
itself fallen quickly in competing gusts.
Why the grass should succumb to such
a covering was a mystery to us all.

II.

She grabbed my hand as we headed
off on the path above the sea, by the
commemoration bench for one whose
favourite place it was to sit and watch.

III.

Perhaps the eagle will simply grasp
the burning cross and carry it high
above the village. Perhaps the embers
will then fall on those who look up.

from FROM THE EVIDENCE (2018)

THE DEPOSITION AND ROLLING AWAY OF THE STONE

after Stanley Spencer

The need for geometries, correct
instrumentation; the body aligned
precisely, pinned and mounted
on wood with right hammer

and good nails. Then the taking
down: how one might stoop
to the task, squint into the flesh
to get the exact purchase, which pliers

would extract the nails most effectively,
how to lever and jemmy appropriately.
And the sounds of it all, how the nails
squeeze from the wood, the flesh

slipping off the upright, the feet
with their slight *whoosh* of parting,
anticipation of stone rolling upon
stone at the entrance to the tomb.

HANG GLIDERS WITH SAXOPHONES

The saxophones circle in the air
above the moor, the thermal column
that the breath supports.

Keys rest neatly on the pads,
pads rest neatly on the air,
one and two and three and four fingers

supporting wings above the Earth.
Between sky and crushing ground,
they overblow the octave, one to another:

sopranino and baritone,
alto, bass and tenor,
soprano, too; Roland Kirk's

manzello, stritch. Levers
and rods hold taut the bell for air;
in early autumn heat with rooks

and crows careening in the blue.
Sonny Rollins – 'Saxophone Colossus'
on up-draft wings, black flaking

against the sky, his poignant sound
above the peat drift and the craquelure
of moorland, maggoty with sheep.

FROM THE EVIDENCE

i. The Parachute

is listening to the air beneath its feet,
the ground rush, the earth spread,
cloud urging the horizon,

as river urges the bridge,
bridge flowing, hand repressing
water and wind that ripples

the jumpsuit. Cold gathers
over skin, eyes in goggles, weighs
time between two brass pans

of scales, one past, one present, the future
swooping low, a dark cormorant
over sea and estuary, tent and tall building.

ii. The Keyhole

Had the keyhole not forced its way inside
the apple, having pushed the pith
and juice aside, beneath the padlock

of the tree, its shackle and lockbar,
each part calling to the other in the arc
of tree, would the storm have built

around it, beading an abacus of lightning
that rattles its rods to frame
the keyhole in the ghost of an apple?

iii. The Trouser Role

The rainbow is, as ever, in the trouser role,
wears spats, slides down itself, in top hat
and tails; its cane, ebony with an ivory handle

and brass ferrule, taps out magic, gains
battles in vain, might bend itself around
the whole world, end up wafted in fountain

spray, the droplets each footprinting
rainbow, eliding the shine of wedding ring,
lorgnettes held up to the light but

incurably smeary with rainbow
sliding further into the fountain,
the old hoofer, variegated vaudevillian!

iv. Holding your nerve

Light encroaches on the eyelid, the yellow
atoms mix with shadow round the eye,
even to the optic nerve. Like the pheasant

on the lawn, in feathered knee-britches,
lifting his naked ankles, keratinous talons,
who might rouse himself to a brief keratinous

shout that moves out over all the atoms
of the motorway, and is, in fact, two masks
that peel apart, the inside looking out

and the outside looking out, a set of
ruined crenellations pulled down one
by one from off the top of a tower

which overlooks a gaunt estuary;
the optic nerve chafes inside
the socket, scheming its way to the light.

v. Stabat Mater

Giovanni Batista Pergolesi inside
the tent of his tuberculosis, his
lungs yawing on gimbals, watches

the canvas door stir open, show all
the night of stars…*fount of love –*
feel sorrow deep as yours – mourn

with you …He is our ghost, tilts us up,
in turn, towards each compass point
of light, that flows beneath the several

bridges, the rainbow of the globe's
encompassing horizon, which makes
the wound of earth, the caul of sea.

vi. My present is surely

The rooks must learn to sleep in the same air,
and see that ring of stars flock out from off their
pedestal, whose time is a task that treads from

leaf tip to leaf tip, in the gaps between time,
who trail their feet in flight between the branches,
their cries flaking and falling from rookery to roost,

for when the lightning reaches from the sky
to touch a spire, the white noise rising and
falling, the wet grass cut in rucks and gathers.

vii. Rhubarb

The rhubarb is heaving air into its lungs,
hands on knees, red face towards the pavement.
The fountain of its leaf is magnetised to point

towards and shelter from the gibbous moon,
that marathon store of light that's sucked deep
into the lungs, the masks that Aristotle writes,

like the cochineal derived from the exoskeleton,
like the empennage pitching and yawing,
like the filament heaving light into the air.

viii. Lanolin

The sheep breathes normally; its inhalation and exhalation
moving over mucus membrane in its nose. So the sheep's
cloven feet tread on the grass, its teeth crop grass, wear, chip,

are not uniform, where the feet are sure and unimposing.
The stone work of the bridge arches to the river, whose
water washes ripples back and across the stone. Whose

water washes the dot on the face of the die, the dots on
the face of the die, with the water pirling. Over the clock face,
then, the hand moves, and above the clock, a vapour trail

is firstly sharp, then spreads across the surface of the
postcard which is sky-silk, which billows into rest, as
the gestures that accompany will settle and breathe normally.

ix. The High Vernacular

Where broom has had no flowers, all the summer
is speculation, that walks into the early morning wood
as rain falls through the canopy of leaves above us,

ready there to free small woodland mammals,
bank voles, wood mice, from the traps we've laid
the previous night, bright eyes and perfect ears.

Ivy falls upon the wall. Each leaf flames a keyhole
on each falling stem, a bead upon the rod of its
own abacus, the swing of each pan of the balance.

x. Water nowhere visible

But each an exact texture, the first, slime,
cold, yes, but deft and strong even on hands
of men who handle it. And then, those

fine feet that would not hover further from
a meniscus that would clutch and bring
that pure beast into a set of wild gyrations,

the surface a vibration of locked-in dying.
It might go on to drift, under the autumn;
trees, too, drifting as the wind speeds up;

As if some crossing of the species barrier
would open a vein like a road lying across
a map from the coast to the county border.

xi ...and all that therein is

In the corner, the eye, watching from
inside its veil, sees the wave-work,
the way waves break on the tent of the sea

and all that therein is. Intelligence bodied
in that form unlocks the updraft of the albatross
that, skip, skip, skip, dimples the heave

and carry of the wave and spume.
Wave-drive and albatross-carry caught
as the sea-tent flaps and flicks towards

the eight corners of the globe; eyelashes
dripping brine, the eyelid closing,
the eye, in safety, sheltering behind.

xii. Genre Painting

The fingers touch the spinet, its ivory keyboard.
The choice is ceramic or cloth; there's nothing else.
And so, it will be an apple, then, at lunch.

Details picked out in white lead; how small they are,
men, women, children alike, The whole uproarious
lot of them, particularly those at the back.

It will be the air soaked and the ropes sodden. The boat
rising on the wave, the sea weed too; oars in drenched rowlocks.
Thumb deep in the fish's mouth, finger hooked around its gills.

xiii. The Sea is an Ordinary Room

We are kneeling, listening to staccato adumbrations
of the air and the surrounding silence, the dust
that tips it. How the fingers long to wait inside

the light, their whirled tips wrinkling
in the pressured sea. It is this love of swaying sound
that moves the hands as if in water over

tautened strings, the tuning pegs and fretboard.
From each string, a group of notes is rising,
as the fingernails elicit pitch. The lute, the Chinese lantern,

the flute, the bow and sympathetic strings are like
a chalice falling through towards the sea floor;
each pebble of it separate and smooth, sucked

and rolled within the water's maw, as if a submarine
approached, to light blind fish, crustaceans,
the carapaces and antennae that roam the mud and sand.

HUGHENDEN

In the café with the artificial Ficus
and wrought iron chairs, the girl
who operates the till keeps
asking, 'Is that everything?'

The tree beside the window is alive
with black caps until suddenly it isn't.
The dog in the coach yard,
bounces as it barks. Beside

a monkey puzzle tree, a mother
with a push chair, her children
tumbling on the lawn, which has
a dark, irregular line where foxes

might have run between the caryatids
and beds of cyclamen and pansies.
His rooms so perfectly proportioned,
portraits line the stairs, and,

on his writing desk, a marble copy
of his wife's right foot.
Eight labourers from the estate
bore his coffin to the church.

from SPILLWAY (2020)

SPILLWAY

You went to lie down to examine the root of the tree,
how it came from the earth, as if it were your tree,

your earth. A stand of poplars waited at the field corner
by the pond, the sky a kind of grease. And water

ran over the spillway, water turned on an edge
and rounded, most of the time, in calm weather,

like the hollow into which the axle fits, 'delimited
by a ring of questions' Barth says, questions which

will never cease, so you lay there, spilling and
spinning. It didn't seem like a question, the body

weighted across the ground, the peculiar mirror
of it and what you saw in it, which looked at roots,

then glanced up at the slippery sky, at the crows
sliding across it, perhaps between rookery and roost.

CRAWL SPACE

The railway track divides
where the road slopes up

beside a genteel, Georgian
terrace. Where do we doubt

what this all means, the water
settling behind the swimmer,

as if the body encroached, wanted
to talk, then spread its sleep?

FORGIVENESS

What is it, then, for the clouds to open and
let the sun through; too easy, too objective,

waiting for some contrail to cross the blue
and show that there is one idea moving to

another, a chorus which meets out beyond
the lozenges of stained glass as they parade

along the inside of the church, through which
we might have seen the trees sway and rock,

the tide recede, rocks exposed, a whole new
island that forgives us from the shallow water?

IN CONSEQUENCE

Between this land and the next,
seasons changed, water dried

and footpaths came; past late
August buddleia, its flowers

rusting, to that river, which
had been culverted for one,

and died for another whose hand
dipped into its stream, whose fingers,

ringless, measured the flow, felt for
how it had slid from the hillside.

IF I WOKE IN THE SUMMER NIGHT

If I woke in the summer night, and found
myself like a collared dove descending onto

the moonlit lawn, the stars perfectly placed
around their chosen figures, artificially small,

perhaps, and mostly, as though kneeling before
that anonymous Virgin and Child, the face

of the Virgin bruised and unfinished, putti
seemingly head and shoulders only, their wings

close but only sketched in vague gestures,
the Virgin's drapery that ever-present Prussian blue,

the undifferentiated air might still be gathering,
the whole night round a constellated blue, and,

to the small creature I found drifting past, I would say,
'Bring me luck, little spider, on your flying thread.'

OUR BOOK

Your shadow moving on in front
as if upon a lead, the lights quietly

going down, with the drip of reason
onto ritual. It freights our book

with an autumn Saturday afternoon,
wind spinning leaves from trees

to hedgerows. A cat, in silence, pads
from one place to another. The *meltemi*

spreading light across a choppy sea
is a thought that moves across

the Mediterranean, the body unexamined,
to a house that's built on the edge of sunset.

RAIN

A lexicon of words that were not
said in childhood, and all of those

that were, were said beside
an upturned boat, the lapped

planking of the creosoted shed,
were said into the wind on

tussocky ground, by farm-rust vehicles.
The buildings I could not complete

without my father's help, the wind
in which I was at sea. Rain blooming

in August that moved the land
and over land toward the autumn,

sliding through the gates of summer,
feeling for the bone inside the wrist.

THAT LIGHT

An evening sun that breaks
through clouds, a grey that

banks up across the hills and
from which snow falls almost

vertically; the livid world
in which we might mature,

prepare others for presences;
trampled ground, forests, a few stars.

WHENEVER I SUPPOSE

Whenever I suppose myself near
and see the lamb lie down away

from the ewe, when the shadows
spill into a darker stain, when I speak

of such things, my breath clamouring
beside the swart canal, its brick-work

graffitied, the rows of gas canisters
with their bulbous threat, whenever

I speak of these things, my breath
is a honking skein with illusions

of migration, like flatbeds pent up
in the shunting yard, the piles

of aggregate ready to slide,
elder with its scruffy bloom.

IN MEMORIAM DUPREE BOLTON

That time at dusk. The barn owl
beats up and down beside

the meadow fence; sluggish
as if not confident, an aphorist

of predation. Its flat, wide face
divided about the beak,

its beautiful cruelty divined
from wit, made righteous

in progeny, the plurality of
individuals, meaning one.

As when we see the bodies
of animals at the roadside

and know that birds have
flown above them, filled

with a power that was most
intimately theirs and not them.

NEW POEMS

1969

The camera focused
on a woman

in the doorway
closest to the barricade,

who must now be dead;
a life as determined

as that of the man
moving from the edge

to the centre, towards
the soldiers bent

over tiers
of torn-up paving.

THE GARDEN

In that walled garden, beside the path,
espaliered plum trees stretch on the breeze,

on steel wires. The sun drifts round
what ripens and winds, that connect

post with post and calm desire. So when
and if the soul has sudden appetites,

when we are impatient to be only ourselves,
partial shelter comes from the worn brick wall.

ASPIRATION 1939

The land breathes sleep among
the creatures. The land a pillow

with trees settled on it where
grain silo and hay barn settle

too, where even the evictions
of the winter night swim with

a kind of grace, yoking old earth
and new, below flat clouds.

On the street, windows highlighted
and, beneath them, a fire hydrant.

The figure at the gas pump is caught
in light from the shop; an upturned

chair balances on upturned stool,
winter air so clear, the light even.

BAPTISM

1.

When you have grown up in a house,
and know the neighbours and have
stood in the orchard waiting for

autumn, with moonlight dividing
the sky, pavements dry, and shelves
of the back-street shops over-full,

you might just stand in the warm
river, or simply pass round bread
and feel the arguments come and go.

2.

When the brick-work becomes
important, and then the wall,

perhaps the river will help us,
offering its taut surface

and mild depth, in the way
that a horse so loves

the alien taste of peppermint,
or molasses rubbed on the bit.

BETRAYAL

Bronze and messy among
the fallen acorns, but also

seeming to bend away,
becoming, edge on, dots

and notes enmeshed and
overlapping, or just a line,

but fleshly, as though repulsed
by himself, aghast at the

rulings of the spirit, showing
how far betrayal has proceeded

in him, the masculinities
distorted and mottled.

DESERT

I am walking away as into a desert. The trees on the left-hand side
and the wall in the left-hand corner give me a sense of depth. I would

rather the willow leaf fall was painted with dry brush scumbling, to darken
the colours towards the diagonal line, as if to create some sense of shade,

but on the other side of that line I and my canvas are blank. I had wanted
to open out the canvas and sit on the swaying, striped resistance of its chair.

I could then have blended in with my mother's garden, with the peaches
darkening to pulp above me, and kumquats trickling onto the soil. She

might have had persimmons, but instead she had me, my insubstantiality
dancing around her memory, the horizon crazed with swaying palm trees.

WHITE ONYX LINE

after Richard Long: Whitworth Art Gallery, Manchester, 2013

We might be a canoe at the head of the river,
at the point of portage, the sharp edge and

the blurred edge, dark edge and the light.
When I saw the earth breaking, when I saw

the still rocks moving, when they were
followed by plug points and cables, an aerial

for terrestrial TV, cabling for the land line,
a faux classical head in bas relief above the door,

then net curtains, a doorbell black on white,
the paint falling as water falls, streaking the facia,

the stucco and the pigeon roof, the sightlines
perfect, gantries and lighting rigs, then I felt

the rocks rub over my hands, front and back,
and the sky seep into my eyes. The pressures

of air weighed down upon the earth; white onyx
ran from one occluded slope to another,

when the clouds came over, nearly touched
the hills, and the house translucent and

transfigured, emerged like a great, contorted fish.

DARK WATER

There was a drop of water,
from a splash of water,

which came to rest on the
dark pine of the table top,

where my finger pushed
the water on the dark surface,

under trees, and my heart beat
felt, through the walls

of my chest, like a dog
panting as the sun sets.

Not long after this, he asks, 'What then
are we?' which he answers with, '*Sin*

burst into life. [His italics]. But, sometimes,
I wonder if sin is his real interest, as, just

afterwards, he writes, 'Death is the mark
of that passing of eternity into time which is,

of course, not an occurrence in time, but
a past happening in primal history,' as if

that were played in the left hand, the time
seemingly vague in the right hand, where

the wood of the piano encasement holds
the music, time held in its grain, the air

above the piano, calm and unruffled, like
a bridge rising, the boat moving towards it.

A DROVE ROAD

That he studied their elements before
he went among them, as if to run

his hand down the branches and
smooth the leaves into a single

direction, is less important if
we understand that he was not alone,

that they had already borrowed
necessary sacraments, the path

an old drove road up through
brambles and Himalayan balsam,

the stones displaced and uncertain
underfoot, over the hill, where larks

did, actually, rise into grey skies and,
across the valley, fast trains passed

as if behind a wooden screen, their
clattering echoing over sloping fields.

THE BODY

Animals in early morning light
revive a pre-dawn chivalry,

the pigeons on dew-soaked grass,
a white mug of coffee cupped

so we might know the body,
that it engages one, forbids

another; the sun shining
as if through paper, tender and slow.

FORESHORTENING

Breathing is often outside the face,
just out of reach of the mouth;

like gaze which is, itself, memory,
like a shadow which falls across

a darkened doorway. And those
fingers, with their large gold rings,

that flick open a brass cigarette lighter,
they, too, are just beyond reach.

Continuation is both waiting
and surprise, as if he stood to see

both beermats and moorland heather
in the wall mirror of the pub.

GIVERNY

Summer dust settled over the garden
in bloom and full of bees; their hives

full of such marketable honey, you
bought a jar. Then, amid the light blue

and white of the ground floor, there was
the lemon-yellow room and the room

in two pale blues with a Hiroshige carp
and a falcon, its talons folded under

because the hands were difficult, though
worked on over some days, and the neck

difficult, the edges of the object fleeing
towards the horizon, fleeing the unity

of flesh and (that word again!) spirit; so,
perhaps it <u>was</u> easier to leave the eyes out

altogether, as in the small Cezanne upstairs,
where the face is wide and slightly empty.

The features caught in the shadow of an
overhang. Outside the leaves fell from bamboo

in the Japanese water garden, leaves that
gathered light grey stripes upon light green stripes

and the stream that ran between pinioned banks,
as if we had opened a desk marked by all

who had used it, who had slept in its dust,
who had slept in the dew in the summer.

WORK

In the half-light, we can hardly see the canvas:
birds on the canal are green on green, the edges

of wings are divots in the brushstrokes; yellow
dawn-light reaches across the chemical works,

puddles lit, dotted with rain, and, beyond them,
the ochre café, alive with those who wait to work.

THE MAP CHEST

And as I bent over the large top
of the map chest to tidy folders,

papers, plastic wallets, the window
rose above me; across the valley,

green meadows fell, a church,
half-hidden, shouldered out onto

the skyline, its curt brickwork
pitted with windows like light bulbs

waiting for the filament to burn out.
And when the map chest

was tidy and relocked, and when
the church was spilled as if its flesh

were sand, the rain came over the hill,
like water blown over the heel

of my hand, the hand that was no good
there, and no good anywhere else.

A MOVEABLE FEAST

But Paris was a very old city and we were young and nothing was simple
there, not even poverty, nor sudden money, nor the moonlight, nor right and
wrong, nor the breathing of someone who lay beside you in the moonlight.
Hemingway, *A Moveable Feast*

That time, the Danube canal was full and moving fast,
not that we went out to the river to compare them, except
at Stift Melk, where everything was gold and you bought me

that small pot of abbey honey that I only just finished
three years later. And when we arrived in the evening,
the swifts filled the air and the next day, there were none,

so I thought perhaps they were on their way through and
we had caught them on their way to the Mediterranean.
The next night, though, I sat on the balcony and there they

were again, in the increasingly overcast sky. After the notes
had been brought up from the Ritz basement twenty-six years
later in a trunk that Vuitton had made especially for him,

he wrote that Tatie and Hadley reminisced about 'sitting
on the porch, drinking Sion wine and eating freshly cooked
trout, with the mountainside dropping off below.'

OBVIOUS THINGS

Beyond the window, cow parsley
shines in and through itself along

the green canal and those walking
on the towpath beside the boats.

Summer drifts unseasonably;
evening turns the tide of light

over fern, a stand of birch saplings
where lichen inscribes slate.

And I might have bent to smell
the lichen, pushed my face into it,

snuffling, absorbing what it means
to become unclothed in death.

HORIZON

Much as we might want it,
these things cannot be undone,

like that young man, there,
who leans against the wall

of the house. And we, who
imagine ourselves above such

things, whose grandparents
grew apricots and gathered

honey, whose graves we tend
and plant with vine tomatoes,

are dragged back, fearful
as much as anything;

the windows blown out,
the brick-work blackened.

RAVENNA

The shoulder turned towards you,
the button-through just visible,

with its impacted threads.
A preparation for arrival, a message

that is shared, which asks also, prays
even, for support, like a belt tightening

across my chest, my stubby fingers
pushing under it. Those apprehensions

of the past have cast a shadow; water
drips from the blade of the oar, the stroke

of the blade on the surface, each purling circle
where the river retreats from the oarsman.

SHIBBOLETH

To sort the sheep of his
supporters from the goats
of Ephraimites, Jephthah
made his enemies speak
the word for ears-of-wheat;
the voiceless palato-alveolar
fricative 'sh', their lips and
tongue just could not
frame. The check-points
of the 'Ears-of-wheat' found
and killed so many. But later,
round the sand-cleaned
table tops, the beer pots
and the spillage, under
the reed weave shade,
cooled by a purling wind,
filled with fermentation from
the ears of barley, talk spilled
to the edges of the field,
the burdens of the ass, how
the winnow and the flail
will wrest the kernel
from the chaff. They
tested all the tongue
songs that they'd learned:
'Jesting at justice,
Jephthah jeeringly judges,'
or 'Grinning Gileadites
gaily glisten in gore,'
egged each other on
with mad translations

that they knew,
'My timbrels are full
of ears-of-wheat.'
'My ears-of-wheat
explode with desire.'
How they fell about
the two and forty thousands
of the Ephraimites.

Jephthah finally tired
of mortal enemies and
voiceless mispronunciations:
'Oh, that was yesterday's
taboo. We did that one
to death. We all love
Ephraimites today.'

But on his death bed,
when a funerary pulp
of bread was pressed,
for one last meal,
towards his stilling mouth,
did his lips and tongue
form silently around
the word for 'ears of wheat',
those places that his
enemies could not speak,
where two and forty
thousand spirits
would not follow,
until they started
whispering in his
ear, 'Sh, Jephthah, sh'?

BOXES

It was a fiction, a secular judgement,
useful for a time, useful for the time it took

the train to echo along the platform because
he knew the old companies, had known them

after the war and into the fifties; knew
their products, had seen them in large boxes

on shelves, had bought them, divided them
into the old tobacco tins he so carefully

whitewashed, had licked the end of a pencil
and written their names onto the ends of the tins

he shelved in his shed beside the railway;
the train beating the shed with its little rages.

SFUMATO: JOHN SINGER SARGENT

He loved their skin, but
most of all their hands,

against the textured blend
of grey over green; and

their gaze, the set of the
mouth, the set of the eyes,

and, among the lanterns,
all that atonement,

as if the work were
a kind of prohibition.

SHELVES

The woman strode out first, the man
behind, who pulled the luggage,

to take the airport bus through
the suburbs on an Athens' night,

lights on the balconies, lights in the trees.
Like two books with a common subject,

whose authors' surnames start with 'w',
beside each other on the shelves:

the former president, who lived above
and brought my letters down

with increasingly bad grace; and her,
who never kissed me all that time.

THE TENT-MAKER: EVANGELISTRIAS MONASTERY, SKIATHOS, SEPTEMBER 2018

to Ben

Paul the apostle, the tent-maker, when needing help took it only where,
it seems, he would not have to give it in return, and so it was that we

turned right past the petrol station, past the port authority building
and beyond it, where, in the uncut verge, three turkeys, a parent

and two youngsters freely grazed, with that strange sound their family
mystery makes, past the summer villas, a playground in a garden,

its swings all chained, sheep crowded in too small a field fed hay by
a man who walked in corduroys among them and, high on the hill,

above both them and us, an unfinished, sharply-pitched roof, all this
in the late afternoon, which was the time we'd chosen, still hot, and you

lagged behind, to watch the many cats, the way their casual lives are worked,
and summer dusty dogs, barking on chains behind dull fences; at the end

of the climb was the stone-built monastery, its plants, succulents
or lemon trees in olive oil cans, a man hosing them as some people

waited for the service in the dark chapel with icon-crusted walls
and close chairs where I bent to see the much-kissed Annunciation,

while you, with your sweet confidence, asked the driver in English
if, when the priest had finished, we could have a lift back down the hill.

THE AERODROME

This is rain in the Home Counties.
It falls on station platforms, on bicycle

helmets, on magpies that strut
on the grass, among the crows that spool

from the tops of trees, and winter
wheat as it appears in the field,

the field corner with its weed and rubbish.
It is raining from the corner all the way

to the horizon, *to where the 'no'*
is divided from the 'yes'; and beyond

to that transfiguration, and to you,
old aerodrome among fields, runways

among grass, broken frames, Nissen huts
that rust among the silver birches.

THE CLAY PIPE

The clay pipe from a ploughed field
is simply another such casualty,

like a human body too attached to
itself, that lives according to sets

of accreted laws, but appears, over time,
to move to a milder, seemingly

less confrontational position, having
had its right to be, contested,

as the air reaches to a horizon that pulls
away from the sea. And in the wave,

bladder wrack, the black egg cases
of skate, jelly fish as toxic alive as when

they are dead and waxy, washed onto
the sand's distorted, elongated gasping.

THE END OF APRIL: IN MEMORY OF MY FATHER

Finally, at the end of April, when
afternoon light was strong enough

to show the yellow of dandelions,
he might have stroked the leaves

of wild garlic, the thin edges buckling,
he might have touched the underside

of butter burr, the soft hooks that live
out of the light; or ferns, new curlicues

growing among the grey; he might have
felt the crisp feathers of the Canada goose

on the canal, stroked the firm back, pushed
down a little, expecting the sanguine body

of the bird to bob back up like a child's toy
on bath water. Except that, towards the end,

having lost the whorls of finger end,
the knuckle, the bone digit that gripped

the pen, the stub that was his forefinger
became too painful to write with;

because these were fingers that had
not escaped, that had formed together

into a shape through which water
and sand flowed with equal measure.

SECRETARIAT

In the big house across the park,
they are watching the blur

of a horse. Famously, it has
three white socks, a sign

of weakness in a horse, who,
when autopsied, had a heart

twice as big as any other.
It is also true, there

is within a voice
its delegate, its impress,

its negativity, a voice that is
very quiet indeed, the hooves

reaching over splashing sand.
And I, myself, who watches

the big house, have a voice
which empties what I give,

empties like a ewer loosing
its blurring reach of water.

HIDDEN IN THE FIELDS OF ASPHODEL

They might stand and smile, greet each other,
the conversation settle into seriousness,

come down from the upper decks into the corridor,
come down into the sound of engines, oil smell,

petrol and sea, revelations, too, beneath the layers
of metal, the ultrasound exploring it all,

as you might emerge on the beach from the sand
your child has buried you in, as the seaweed

appears at low tide, the tide water falls, not drying.
And on that self-same strand, the two of them

walk towards us, paper blowing across their path.
Where we might be repulsed by them, we are attracted

by the spirit, like the blackbird that sings for a mate
well into the spring, as the tree fills with leaves.

THE RAILWAY CHILDREN

Even the countryside is recalcitrant;
the train those children wave to

threads its shadowy impress towards
a series of incompletions; and from

the summer garden emerges the unity
of the one spirit and the one body,

its hands clenched and the mouth firm.
And always someone else there, echoing

across the grass, echoing near the wire fence;
like the climbing roses, all realism and

logic as they move in the air, pink with
petals that crisp at their black edges.

SHINGLE STREET

Wooden pilings rose from the tidal river.
The sky descended, pushed us out

to the margins, and I became a sightless,
sighing thing who flew the huge, open

cave of sky, above a tractor whose pipework
and tyres sliced the earth. The words,

'too late, too much', flat and uninflected
as a small cloud crossing the sun, bundled

over the newly turned soil. And seagulls,
each made a fragment, followed the tractor.

TREE TOPS

In blue, autumn sky, the yellow
dot of a sunlit plane moves between

tree tops, the flat beside the railway
line looks through trees to the building

on the other side, to that community
of sky light, although the music is lost,

birdsong where the beat has stilled,
green fields, whose rhythm is that shell.

UNTITLED IV

The old men become younger when
they paint, those commuterland houses

stretch away from the railway
towards the farm land; that dog

and its owner there beyond the apple tree
with the blue trunk, nasturtiums in shadow,

emitting light. The light rises to the left,
flames up and away over pots of peonies,

the trellis and arch of trailing flowers,
over the dormer window in a pantiled roof.

WHAT THE CAMERA SAYS

The shadow of the camera
catches the unease in your face.

Behind you, mountains stretch
towards the pale entry

of the moon looking down in daylight.
The mountains offer snow

towards the sun, as if the moon
were an embarrassment.

saw Mingus fire his pianist
mid set, the smoke curling from

the bassist's cigar; saw Mingus'
redemption amid spotlights

and the hush, and memorialized
Mingus' death as like the beaching

of whales. How the horns
of Brown and Dolphy cut against

the chords, and felt the tune
haul them against it; the clarity

of the recording such, it is
the bassist who comes across most clearly.

A GULL BESIDE MOVING CARS

Those houses, that are haunted, are most still
Webster, *The Duchess of Malfi*

A one dollar note that was used
as a bookmark in Carl Phillips'

Selected *Quiver of Arrows* moved
mysteriously to Barth's *Epistle*

to the Romans and became a knife
used for cutting and for

marking time; its strange eye
looking out as if to justify

the sound of scaffolding as
it falls, upended onto the pipe

ends that slaps flat along the length
of pipe onto the pavement then

rolls onto the road, unchecked,
or like a gull on the pavement

beside the road with moving cars
that keeps turning its head into

the breeze, the gull's feathers
pushed open momentarily.

TODAY

The boat moored away from the bank,
needing a dinghy to get to the bank;

a man sat calmly on the grey cabin roof,
watched the river emptied of dinghies.

Among the river bank reeds, a man sat,
self-absorbed, watched the tiller push,

even at anchorage. After the storm,
all was idyll, raindrops ran off leaves,

cattle stood up to their knees in the river,
the boy's dog stared, ears cocked,

pigeons on branches, mooring ropes
slack. Then into this, a woman walked,

heavy coat and woollen hat, who walks
the same direction in the morning,

in the evening. Today, I saw her
in the market, small roads, wide sky.

A MAP

the ripple in a brook-warp as gorgeously
blank as a galaxy
A.R. Ammons

It was always like this, that map,
matt grey, matt red, the words

spilling across the colours.
How else could it burrow into

the concrete things of the world,
and look ahead, cigarette ash

falling, the brush moving rapidly
across the canvas, the flat back-

grounds, then further on
toward the lacerating shards,

on which all choices are equally
choices, whose pulses are divided

by white lines, like audio tape un-
spooled across a wooden floor?

BEIRUT

And when the law arrives over
roof tops and summer trees,

and I think of us together in
that bed after thirty years,

it does not mean what brought us
here is how the room will lead us,

like a crane in the warm sky
turned towards the abandoned

gas holder, the ladder up to the
crane driver's cab enclosed in

bright structures, there before
and here now, that avoid the natural

world, and us, who wake from
our small time before the horizon,

like a towel hung to dry on a balcony,
that swells and eddies in the breeze.

MOLTO ANDANTE

But if I turn out the light,
the canal path is no less dark,

the street lights picked out
no less vehemently through

the branches of the trees
tangled as if stumbling;

passing headlights taking
hold of the skirt of the light

to skate with it, the chair back
no less of a shadow;

the fine-grained reach
a passport between us.

LAW

Say it was the dog sniffing
then licking bread crumbs

from the wooden floor,
or the hyacinth performing

its perfumed growth,
determined to see, hear

and touch, from what
indicates to what demands,

in that same place
with the same bodies,

and the smell of rain in
another spring evening.

LOWERING

Up on the flower-laced balcony,
where the monkeys sat, under

a moon like a decal in the blue,
and the contrails like a line

in the blue, they drew their swords.
They lowered the duck, hanging

by one leg; the rabbit, hanging
by one foot, the partridge, hanging

by one foot. And waited for them
to swing against the brick-work

amongst the exhibits, while we
were looking; then we finished

looking, and lowered our eyes,
and the colours changed. Perhaps

when we had taken in all the colours
and the eyes, they, too, would look.

SUBMERGED

The edge of what can be seen was submerged,
dragged, we might say mercifully, beneath

the surface, like the baby turtles that emerged
to run the threats of gulls and surf to meet

the sea their mothers came from, or our eyes
fixed on a factory chimney projected up

against a white sky, otherwise reflected
in the wet street, a resemblance meeting

in the building above and below that feels
now as if knurled against the skin, although

the hand was too large, the finger tips beyond
medicine, bringing about their own cure.

AFTER DEANNA PETHERBRIDGE

Like the rods of an abacus and the beads
that slide repeatedly among them,

that once smelled of the new wood
of an old tree, with the mild rattle of beads

as if among silent bushes, the quick fingertips
trickle over the leaves, over patterns

the sun gives as shadows, like the curtains
flapping over the window sill,

the whole scene stretching obediently,
the whole broad road of it, without

a moment's respite, the whole scene
like the slated jetty with its reach over the water.

TOUCHING THE LIGHT

The eye sees light through the lens
and wants to look up through that

lens and watch the moon in the trees,
the sky dancing. And see this as a child

sees light in the warm bed-time rabbit.
And *if we are content with something less,*

*if we trim and adjust grace so that it
dovetails in with other possibilities* or

the feel of silk inside the lid, feel it
trap the tips of the fingers, let finger tips

move to the fabric hinge, warn them
to sing its praises, *if we do not long for*

*a life running so near that it would visibly
break through*, the finger tips will stall

and words speak like finger tips,
the whorls of the finger tips.

ENTROPIES

In our skin, what we might always be
is like that wash of cloud that layers

and unfixes, in the pronounced body,
in death, in clouds; as on the quay side,

a small, brown dog sniffs among
lobster pots, small dog with no end

in sight, no sense of shame, no falling
outside of it, the end. What we might

always do, flick open a brass lighter,
the soft fizz of the steel wheel, paraffin

smell, and a small part of the skin heated
and itself, is remember how clear water

washes over rocks, the soles of our shoes
trying to grip. And, above the beach,

seed heads nod in the breeze like a group
of people bent over a desk to share a pen and sign.

THE WILLOW CABIN

Yes, the fixed path, the one we needed
to drive the horse down to the shore,

put the seagulls up into the wind, hooves
at a canter all at the same time off the sand

and out there a boat perched like a bird
on the land, the sea brine thick in the wind,

as when geese are strangers to the earth, the cars
below them nothing, the roads below them

nothing, except at night inside the nothing
rain leads them to the watershed and the next river.

OBEDIENCE

If I say that the light from
each round window

gives obedient hatching
to the crosses inlaid in

the floor, that it is
those steps and lines,

those diagonals, that move
precisely one upon another,

and when the meal ends,
each two pairs of hands

help to move the tables,
then I might say my words

begin as an obedience, beside
the grey stone window

frames, and that each word
is first a circlet of bees

upon the evening entrance
to the hive, and then it is

the sound a biplane makes
low over sunlit fields.

ALL THESE THINGS

All these things emerge like stems
from the snow, the white contains

and then releases, the branches
continue and leaves form. And they

will know, the ones who stand
beneath, how the branches move,

how the tip of the tree moves
against the white, the one part

labelled against another, that what
exists is identical with the divine,

and the buckled earth upon which
the unseated root will sit. Details

that leach away so close they have to go,
and the light open on what is suddenly left to us.

THE BEADED EYE

They saw it on an inward eye
no longer the simple thing but

as though, the beetle turned
upon its back, they had splayed

its legs, unveiled the striations
of its shell that tiny and attenuated,

rose, attached to another level,
had emptied the exoskeleton,

then waited in an afterlife, as
if reminiscing, because there

are always things a body needs
to preserve its sanity, antennae,

thorax, spiracles, say, each stencilled
and numbered to preserve our

own illusion of our uncracked
skin, our tear ducts bright and clear.

THE FAINTEST IDEA

I want you to explain how
the end of the building,

the narrow clapboard end,
seems wider when we pass it,

under the cherry blossom,
the window splashed with

dust. It is where a fullness
starts in an empty room that

frees itself from the limitations
we put upon it, and is unlimited

like the smell of the new gloves
in which I listen to you, at your

funeral, the recording of you
accompanying, it seems,

the wicker casket, the container
that dissolves the finiteness

with which it is contrasted, like
the words you walked among,

one foot stopping, then the
other foot stopping, like

the rain that later runs down
windows of an accelerating train.

KITES

Snipe and curlew, the avocet
    on a river dimpling
    under rain,
the dunnock chafing in the ivy.
    So a man travels
    on a dull train,
through cooling Friday towns,

night settling
    around them.
    Red kites above
this Chiltern village
    see a rabbit carried
    from the summerhouse
and are known

to flex and buckle
    stillness on the breeze
    to swoop.
The man above the woman,
    watching her smile,
    the hair sweated
over her forehead.

CHARLOTTENBURG

Even in 40° heat, the whole estate revolves
around the four that sleep in marble beneath

the mausoleum dome, their heads in silent
inclination. As the contingent city spreads

east and north with its shanty-chic, reclaimed
wood, and factory spaces changed to clubs

and indoor skate board parks, inch by inch
of their exterior painted into pictures.

Over Kopernikusstraße, swifts appear and
disappear, a loose mesh one second and hot,

blue sky the next. Over dead grass, as we
walked from the DDR museum that witnessed

East Germans' love of naked, outdoor life, and
its statutory Trabant, along Unter den Linden,

beside the Brandenburger Tor, where IG Metall
in orange T-shirts, gathered their thick accents,

through the Tiergarten beneath low trees, past
stone circles, to emerge in thick heat across the road

and round from the Gemäldegalerie, its bustling
Rembrandts and empty, tabled entrance hall.

If she had not preceded all of that, would she,
in east wind winter, have wrapped herself in furs

to go out through the trees to those four figures
and the stairs that lead down to the crypt, before

she retired to Lietzow after their son was born,
her marital duties done? Or gone out towards

the river, past the gelid carp-pond, where the fish
hearts wait and quieten? Before she too, was

sculpted in stillness, the palace renamed in
her honour, whose marbled head watches the stairs.

THE FALL: AFTER ANSELM KIEFER

The tree emptied itself. The leaves were still
as hands, showed the buildings in winter,
the trees as solid white, the wood
in the air the key to the fields.

I wanted to place these people in such a way
that the light would watch them all, like feet
seen in a pavement skylight; to show
the aeration of the bones, the way the body

calls with its own cry, the head still, waiting,
where the stone disrobes you, gathers
around your feet; the bridge of your nose
flattened as if from pressing too hard at the window.

So the breath grazes on all these pictures,
the pictures breathe back. Inside that hull
are humans. As humans they hang deep
in the rotting sea, the oxygenating, rusting sea.

They work with old hoists and cranes. Using
the machinery lifts them through and into
the sun, where hard hats shine in the sun,
and dust gusts through concrete floors.

Small yellow machines, with black tyres
and wide dusty treads, and sun-splashes
on bonnets and roofs. Straps snag and
frames fold and stack in neat, broken piles,

where sand trickles from shifting plates
and pistons, places in the sand. What does it
mean to work under the sun, under the skin?
Certainly a wheel may need centering,

so brake lights shine at the cross roads.
The road that follows you into the town
and the roads that follow you out, where,
eventually, your eyes give in to the need to sit down.

THE PIED FANTAIL, THE MAGNOLIA

Anyone who submits to his own impulses is bound for trouble
inscription at Loha Prasat temple, Bangkok

Accustomed to live under
corrugated zinc, in transparent houses,
the afternoon is a gated community
of silence and butterflies, finches in
pairs, moving among the leaves, until
the wind and rain return, moving
the world into darkened white noise.

When night falls, the house opposite
is porous with children's screams, the swoop
and fall of intonation, and birdcall like
single, ricocheting stones across the gravel.

*

As it thunders, somewhere among
the bushes, a bird whistles its answer.
Then the rain cascades
and the temperature does not fall,
only rain and the wind falling.
A small crocodile circumspectly swims
in the pale green drainage ditch
beside the veranda. The thunder
runs; lightning holds the sky.
The birds are silent; the butterflies,
huge and solitary, have stopped,
until a moorhen with curved beak
works and reworks the brief storm pool

beneath the trees. The small crocodile
slides from the bank back into the stream.

The bloom of the storm over,
among the foliage, a frog begins
to pink, pink. For a while, we all sit out
experiencing it, the couple in the end room,
the driver in the middle room, and us.
Perhaps, to the driver, I am the silent *farang*
she sleeps with, and what he does not know,
how she kisses me hard on the mouth,
cups the back of my head in her hand,
pulls my face into hers.
So I am glad that she speaks
easily to the others, and I sit outside
knowing our intimacy and how fond
of her I am. In the night, we wake,
entangled and sexless; outside,
cicadas ceaselessly rake gravel.

*

On the Khao San Road,
the Guns and Roses t-shirts
hum along to Coldplay,
and the girl who walks
with a slight limp, a white top
and soft clinging trousers.

The tourist's silent conversation
is with those at home; but
the neighbour asks,
'What does your *farang* eat?'

Breakfast is deep in the hotel area;
Eggs fried in a shallow dish and
heated bread with sugar and 'margarine'.
She draws a map then drives to park.
I cross the street to the fish market.
Many of the fish are still alive;
a catfish moves, its body slashed,
its innards open to the air. Toads
and crayfish move in their nets.
In some cans, there is water.

*

The monastery complex is garish
and crude, the lake fetid and torpid.
In the shallows, snake fish hang
unmoving, terrapins paddle
slowly on the surface. All the fish,
it seems, turn at the surface to gasp
for air. On tiled terrace, in bare feet,
I tread on the headless moth
red ants are scavenging and
carrying noiselessly across the tiles.

It's raining quietly on the temple, on all nine
storeys: the first floor praises rural life,
a mouldering, broken loom, a fish trap,
cabinets with farming implements.
The murals, largely blue and white
with rural scenes; in one, a couple
share a bed, the woman asleep
and the man wielding a large sword.
The floors above have statues
of gold abbots. On the ground floor,

in front of the relic of the Buddha, people
come with 'monk offerings', the women
next to me have toilet rolls for theirs
– 'why not?' she'd say.

*

In sunshine over forested hills,
a stain of clouds rises and falls.
At the temple, on the plate
that describes the lintel,
a spider makes a web.

The mynahs in their cage clean
their mute from their feet;
the family dog is dry, atavistic,
scruffy, testicular. It seems that only
finches squabble in the bush and only
little egrets fish in the salt pan.

The butterflies, black and gold,
come dipping down the far side
of the hedge, round the gate post
to probe the cautious florets
of deep orange on the garden side.

A pair of pied fantails (*Rhipidura javanica*)
- 'The pied fantail ends with three white half dots
on the edge of its tail; most charming and sweet little birds.'
- skitter and play round trees in the garden.
If one is feeding the other, oh, it is difficult
to know which is which as food seems
passed from one to the other before it is swallowed.

*

The Mekong's rushing wide kilometre;
Laos on the far bank,
a thousand miles from the sea.

In the soap operas, everything is
expensive: houses, interiors, clothes,
the strikingly separate heroes and villains;
in early sunshine, father interviews
son beside the wide river
with vegetation flowing;
girl-next-door's with boy-next-door
whose mother's died expansively,
her funeral broadcast over two whole episodes.
The actor playing the girl is only fifteen.
The actors all shed tears with real facility.
Melodrama, expensive interiors
and lashings of winsome, that
and a good shoot-out.

How early the men rise
on a Sunday morning, to sit
on the back of a Hilux with the others,
their heads swathed in towels.
They stand with garlands
of jasmine at traffic lights, or wave
traffic towards them to sell yam,
rice and coconut packed in bamboo,
that's made since five, in the hut
five hundred metres from the highway;
how they run to get the prime spot
in front of the other four.

*

When what I need is to walk
among the trees, look at the leaves,
feel their sharp edges against
my fingertips, tongue, eyelids;
walk deeper,

… like the flower of magnolia
opened upon the tree,
…like magnolia placed
in the pocket of language
to rot, die, lose its scent.
… like magnolia,

listen for the wind
moving the branches, feel the divots
full of water, my trouser legs
soaked, muddied, thin,
my footing fail.

ACKNOWLEDGEMENTS

Acknowledgements are due to the editors of: *Antigonish Review, Berfrois, Cincinnati Review, Griffin on Griffin* ed. Pamela Scobie, *Manchester Review, The North, Plume, PN Review, Poetry, Poetry Ireland Review, Poetry Salzburg Review, Quimera, Stand, Subtropics, The SHop,* and *Warwick Review.* 'Foreshortening' was commissioned by Mark Epstein for the *Age Concerns* exhibition held at the University of Manchester, June 2018.

A number of these poems have been influenced both conceptually and materially by two particular texts: Karl Barth's *The Epistle to the Romans*, trans. Edwyn Hoskins, (Oxford: Oxford University Press, 1968) and Albert Schweitzer's *The Mysticism of Paul the Apostle*, trans. William Montgomery, (Baltimore: The Johns Hopkins University Press, 1998).

*

Particular thanks are due to John McAuliffe for his meticulous editing, and to Chad Campbell, Jim Johnstone, Livi Michael, and Edmund Prestwich for their help with this volume. Additional thanks are due to: A.C. Bevan, Daniel Bosch, Adrian Bucknor, Douglas Crase, Mark Epstein, Emma Handley, Simon Haworth, Evan Jones, Steve Kendall, Sandra Lickorish, Kittima Makgomol, Mario Martín Gijón, Nicholas Murray, Frances Nagel, William Palmer, Ian Parks, Frances Sackett, Peter Sansom, Michael Schmidt, Pamela Scobie, Ruth Sharman, Mary Sullivan, Michael Vince and Chris Woods.